Usborne
Children's Book of
Baking Cakes

Abigail Wheatley

Designed by
Nancy Leschnikoff & Louise Flutter

Illustrated by Jessie Eckel
Photography by Howard Allman
Recipe consultants: Catherine Atkinson & Dagmar Vesely

Contents

Getting started

Baking cakes isn't difficult, as long as you stick to a few basic rules. Before you start cooking, read the recipe to check you have everything you need. Then wash your hands to make sure you don't spread any germs.

Oven temperatures

All ovens are different – yours may cook things more quickly or slowly than the recipe says. If you're using a fan oven, shorten the cooking time or lower the temperature – the oven manual will help you with this.

Cook cakes on the middle shelf of the oven. Only open the oven door when the cooking time is up, or if you think something is burning.

Weighing and measuring

The recipes show two different types of weights. Use either, but don't swap between them. Measure small amounts with spoons, or measuring spoons if you have them.

Ingredients should lie level with the top of the spoon.

Food allergies

If you have a food allergy or intolerance, or are cooking for someone who has, you'll find lots of information in this book to help you.

All the recipes that contain nuts are clearly marked. Often, nuts are optional, and this is also marked. On pages 60-61 you'll also find full allergy advice for each recipe in the book, setting out which recipes are suitable for allergy sufferers, which can be adapted to be allergy-free, and how to adapt them.

Baking basics

The secret of baking is to do exactly what the recipe says – otherwise the cakes might not turn out quite right. Here are some tips to help you bake perfect cakes every time.

Follow the recipe

Always measure ingredients accurately and use the size and shape of cake tin the recipe says.

Is it cooked?

At the end of the cooking time, take the cake out of the oven. Poke the middle of the cake gently with your finger. It should feel firm and springy. If not, bake for 10 minutes more, then test again.

Cooling cakes

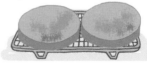

Most cakes need to be left to cool on a wire rack. Wait until the cake is cold before adding fillings and toppings.

Storing cakes

Store your cakes in an airtight container. If they contain fresh fruit, cream cheese or cream, put the container in the fridge. Cakes will keep like this for a few days.

Egg safety

Eating raw eggs can make people ill. Make sure your cakes are cooked, and don't taste uncooked cake mix.

Breaking eggs

Crack the egg sharply on the edge of a bowl. Pull the shell apart, so the white and yolk slide into the bowl. Pick out any bits of shell that fall in.

Beating eggs

Beat the yolk and white with a fork, to mix them.

Separating eggs

Break an egg. Slide the white and yolk onto a plate. Cover the yolk with an egg cup. Hold the egg cup firmly and tip the plate, so the white slides off.

Beating egg whites

Separate the eggs. Beat the egg whites with a metal whisk until they become thick and foamy. When you lift up the whisk, the foam should stay in a floppy point.

Mixing or "folding" in egg whites

Use a big, metal spoon. Move it gently through the mixture, making the shape of a number 8. Stop as soon as it is mixed in.

Butter or margarine

When a recipe says to use softened butter, leave it at room temperature for an hour before you start cooking. You can use soft margarine straight from the fridge.

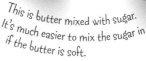

This is butter mixed with sugar. It's much easier to mix the sugar in if the butter is soft.

Little cakes

If you're new to baking, little cakes are simpler to tackle first, as they cook quickly and are easy to handle. Here are some tips to help you.

Muffin trays and cake cases

Most recipes in this section are written for a 12-hole deep metal muffin tray and paper cake cases. If you haven't got any cake cases, just rub the hollows of the tray with a piece of kitchen towel smeared with a little butter.

Using silicone

If you have silicone trays or cases, you can use them instead. Silicone trays work without cases, or being greased, and silicone cases hold their shape on an ordinary baking tray.

A silicone case

A vanilla cupcake

If you're making mini cupcakes, put the paper cases on a flat baking tray.

Creaming

Beating butter and sugar is called creaming. The butter needs to be soft. First, mix the sugar into the butter slowly, then beat as fast as you can, until it is pale and fluffy.

If it's too hard to cream your butter and sugar, fill a clean mixing bowl with hot water. Tip out the water, dry the bowl, then scrape in the mixture and try again.

Other toppings

As well as the fruit toppings and piping decorations in this section, you can find out how to make sugar toppings, chocolate toppings and home-made decorations later in the book.

Allergy-free little cakes

Lots of the little cakes in this section can be made allergy free. There's a full list on page 60.

Adding food dye

When you add food dye, pour it from the bottle onto a teaspoon. If you pour out too much, tip some away. Then, add it to the mixture.

Find out how to make piped toppings and decorations on pages 26-27.

A raspberry macaroon

You can get shiny, metallic cases. Use them like paper cases.

A lemon macaroon

Marbled muffins

Ingredients:

100g (4oz) plain, milk or white
    chocolate in a bar

2 lemons

300g (11oz) self-raising flour

1½ teaspoons of baking powder

125g (4½oz) caster sugar

100ml (4floz) sunflower oil

a little milk

1 medium egg

25g (1oz) cocoa powder

You will also need a 12-hole
    deep muffin tray and 12 paper
    muffin cases

Makes 12

These muffins are made using lemon and chocolate muffin mixtures to create a swirly pattern. There's a chunk of chocolate hidden inside each muffin, too.

1 Heat the oven to 200°C, 400°F or gas mark 6. Put a paper case in each hole of the muffin tray. Break or cut the chocolate into 12 chunks.

2 Grate the zest from the lemons (see page 22). Squeeze the juice from the lemons.

3 Sift the flour and baking powder into a big bowl. Add the sugar and lemon zest and mix.

When you add the milk, the mixture may look lumpy. Don't worry.

4 Put the juice in a jug. Add enough milk to bring it up to the 250ml (9floz) mark. Break the egg into a cup. Beat it with a fork, put it in the jug, add the oil and mix.

5 Pour the contents of the jug into the bowl. Mix quickly with a fork. Stop when there are no lumps of flour left.

6 Pour half the mixture into another bowl. Sift the cocoa powder over it. Mix quickly with a fork.

If you eat these muffins while they're warm, the chocolate will be soft and gooey.

These are plain chocolate chunks, but you could use milk or white if you prefer.

7 Spoon a teaspoon of chocolate mixture into each case. Then, spoon in a teaspoon of lemon mixture. Keep on adding alternate teaspoons, until the cases are a third full.

8 Put a chocolate chunk on top of each one. Cover with alternate teaspoons of the lemon and chocolate mixtures, until they are used up.

9 Bake for 20 minutes, or until risen and firm. Leave them in the tin for 10 minutes, then put them on a wire rack to cool.

Other flavours

To make chocolate and orange or chocolate and lime marbled muffins, replace the lemons with 2 oranges or 3 limes.

Little banana cakes

Ingredients:

125g (4½oz) softened butter or soft margarine

150g (5oz) soft dark brown sugar

2 large eggs

1 teaspoon of vanilla essence

4 large, ripe bananas

250g (9oz) self-raising flour

½ teaspoon of baking powder

1 teaspoon of lemon juice

For the cream cheese frosting:

50g (2oz) icing sugar

200g (7oz) full-fat cream cheese, at room temperature

1 tablespoon of lemon juice

You will also need:

a 12-hole deep muffin tray and 12 paper muffin cases

walnut pieces or extra banana, to decorate, if you like

Makes 12

These little cakes contain fresh banana, which makes them moist and juicy. The riper the bananas, the more flavour your cakes will have. You can make these cakes dairy-free – see the instructions on page 60. The nuts are optional.

1 Heat the oven to 180°C, 350°F or gas mark 4. Fill the tray with paper cases.

2 Put the butter and sugar in a big bowl. Beat them together until the mixture is pale and fluffy.

3 Break an egg into a cup, then put it in a small bowl. Do the same with the other egg. Add the vanilla essence. Mix with a fork.

4 Put a spoonful of the egg in the big bowl. Beat it in well. Add the rest of the egg, a spoonful at a time, beating well each time.

5 Peel the bananas and put them in a bowl. Mash them with a fork or potato masher. Mix in the lemon juice. Tip the mixture into the big bowl and mix it in.

6 Sift the flour and baking powder over the mixture. Mix it in well.

7 Spoon the mixture into the cases. Bake for 20-25 minutes, or until browned and firm.

8 Leave the cakes for 5 minutes, them put them on a wire rack and leave them to cool.

9 Make the cream cheese frosting (see page 51). Spread it over the cakes. Decorate with slices of fresh banana or walnut pieces, if you like.

Topping tip

If you're decorating your cakes with banana slices, mix them in a bowl with a tablespoon of lemon juice first. This will stop them turning brown.

These cakes taste delicious even without a topping.

Vanilla cupcakes

Ingredients:

175g (6oz) self-raising flour
175g (6oz) soft margarine
175g (6oz) caster sugar
1 teaspoon of vanilla essence
3 medium eggs

For the buttercream:
100g (4oz) softened butter or
    soft margarine
225g (8oz) icing sugar
1 tablespoon of milk
1½ teaspoons of vanilla essence
a few drops of food colouring

You will also need a 12-hole
    deep muffin tray and 12 paper
    muffin cases

Makes 12

These pretty cupcakes are topped with buttercream tinted in pastel shades. You can spread the buttercream onto the cakes, or pipe it on in swirly patterns using a piping bag or gun.

1 Heat the oven to 180°C, 350°F or gas mark 4. Put a paper case in each hole in the tray.

2 Sift the flour into a large mixing bowl. Add the margarine, sugar and vanilla essence.

3 Break the eggs into a cup, then pour them into the bowl. Stir until you have a smooth mixture.

5 Bake for 20-25 minutes, or until firm and golden on top.

4 Spoon the mixture into the paper cases, dividing it evenly between them.

6 Leave the cooked cakes in the tray for a few minutes. Then, put them on a wire rack to cool. Meanwhile, make the buttercream (see page 51).

7 When the cakes are completely cool, spread or pipe on some buttercream (see pages 26-27 for piping instructions).

A mini cupcake with a small piped swirl

You could decorate your cupcakes with small sweets or sugar sprinkles.

This buttercream was spread on with a knife.

This cupcake has a piped swirly topping.

Mini cupcakes

Use the recipe for butterfly cakes on pages 24-25: follow steps 1-2, spoon the mixture into the cases and bake for 10-12 minutes. Then, follow steps 6-7 here, to cool and decorate them.

Orange drizzle cupcakes

Ingredients:

3 oranges

175g (6oz) softened butter
or soft margarine

175g (6oz) caster sugar

3 medium eggs

1½ teaspoons of gluten-free
baking powder

165g (5½oz) fine cornmeal
(polenta)

For the orange glacé icing:

175g (6oz) icing sugar

You will also need a 12-hole
deep muffin tray and 12 paper
muffin cases

Makes 12

These moist, tangy cupcakes are made using cornmeal (polenta) instead of flour, which means they are wheat-and gluten-free. You can also make them dairy-free – see page 60 for instructions.

1 Heat the oven to 190°C, 375°F or gas mark 5. Put a paper case in each hollow of the muffin tray.

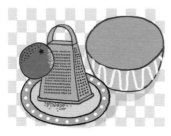

2 Grate the zest from the oranges (see page 22). Put it in a big bowl.

3 Squeeze the juice from the oranges. Put 1½ tablespoons of juice in a bowl and the rest in a jug.

4 Put the butter or margarine and caster sugar in the bowl with the zest. Beat until the mixture is pale and fluffy.

5 Break an egg into a small bowl. Beat it with a fork. Tip it into the big bowl and mix it in. Do the same with the other eggs.

6 Put the baking powder and cornmeal in the bowl. Add one tablespoon of orange juice from the jug. Mix gently.

7 Spoon the mixture into the paper cases. Bake for 20 minutes, until golden and firm.

8 Carefully pour the juice from the jug over the hot cakes. Leave them in the tin to cool.

9 Use the juice you put in the bowl earlier to make the orange glacé icing – see page 38.

10 Scoop up some icing. Hold the spoon over a cake. Tip the spoon, then move it over the cake, leaving a trail of icing.

For drizzling, you need to use quite runny glacé icing.

These cupcakes had extra grated orange zest sprinkled on top.

Lemon or lime drizzle cupcakes

Replace the oranges with 3 lemons or 6 limes.

Chocolate orange cupcakes

At step 5, use just 125g (4½oz) cornmeal and sift 40g (1½oz) cocoa powder into the bowl too. Instead of the icing, melt 100g (4oz) chocolate and drizzle it over the top – see page 56 for how to do this.

Strawberry shortcakes

Ingredients:

For the shortcakes:
225g (8oz) self-raising flour
1 teaspoon of baking powder
50g (2oz) butter
25g (1oz) caster sugar
1 medium egg
5 tablespoons of milk
½ teaspoon of vanilla essence
extra milk, for brushing

For the filling:
225g (8oz) strawberries
150ml (¼ pint) double or whipping cream

You will also need a round cutter around 6cm (2½ in) across

Makes 10

Shortcakes are similar to scones. These are filled with cream and strawberries, but there are suggestions for other fillings on the opposite page. Only fill as many as you want to eat straightaway – you can store the rest.

1 Heat the oven to 220°C, 425°F or gas mark 7. Use a paper towel to wipe a little butter over a baking tray.

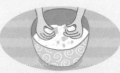

2 Sift the flour and baking powder into a big bowl. Cut the butter into chunks. Stir them into the flour.

3 Use the tips of your fingers and thumbs to pick up some butter and flour, and squash and rub them together. Carry on doing this.

4 The lumps of butter will gradually get smaller and smaller. Keep on rubbing until they are the size of small breadcrumbs. Then, stir in the sugar.

Turn the dough around a quarter of the way each time you roll over.

5 Break the egg into a cup. Add the milk and vanilla. Mix with a fork, then pour into the big bowl.

6 Use a blunt knife to cut through the mixture again and again, to mix it. It will cling together. Pat it into a ball with your hands.

7 Dust a clean work surface with flour. Put the dough on the flour. Roll over the dough, turn it around and roll over it again, until it's 1cm (½ in) thick.

Sift a little icing sugar over the top of the finished shortcakes.

8 Cut out lots of rounds. Put them on the tray. Squash the scraps together, roll them out again and cut more rounds.

9 Brush a little milk onto each round. Bake for 10-12 minutes, until risen and golden brown. Move to a wire rack, to cool.

Pull out the green part, like this, or cut it out if it's hard to pull.

10 Remove the green stalks from the strawberries. Cut the strawberries into thin slices.

11 Whip the cream (see page 50). Cut each shortcake in half, like this.

12 Spread some cream on each lower half. Top with strawberry slices. Spread on more cream. Put the top halves back on.

Other fruit fillings

Replace the sliced strawberries with the same weight of raspberries, blackberries or blueberries. Or, use 3 sliced peaches or nectarines, 2 sliced pears or a small can of pineapple chunks, drained.

Whoopie pies

Ingredients:

75g (3oz) butter

1 large egg

150g (5oz) caster sugar

150ml (¼ pint) carton
  of soured cream

2 teaspoons of vanilla essence

3 tablespoons of milk

275g (10oz) plain flour

¾ teaspoon of bicarbonate of soda

For the buttercream filling:

50g (2oz) butter, softened

100g (4oz) icing sugar

1 teaspoon of vanilla essence

Makes about 12 pairs

Whoopie pies are from America. They are round, flat sponge cakes sandwiched together with buttercream or other fillings. Their name is supposed to have come about because people enjoyed eating them so much, they shouted 'whoopie!'

1 Heat the oven to 180°C, 350°F, gas mark 4. Line 2 large baking trays with baking parchment (see page 30).

2 Put the butter in a small pan. Heat gently until the butter just melts. Take it off the heat.

3 Break the egg into a big bowl. Add the sugar. Whisk for 2-3 minutes, until the mixture is thick and pale.

To decorate a pie with piped icing, see pages 26-27.

4 Add the melted butter, soured cream, vanilla and milk. Mix them in gently using a big metal spoon, moving it in the shape of an 8.

5 Sift the flour and bicarbonate of soda over the mixture. Mix them in gently.

Chocolate whoopie pies

At step 5, use just 225g (8oz) flour and put 50g (2oz) of cocoa powder in the sieve at the same time.

Use another spoon to push each blob off.

6 Put heaped teaspoons of the mixture on the trays, making sure the blobs are well spaced out. Bake for 10-12 minutes, or until golden and just firm.

7 Leave on the trays for 5 minutes. Then, put them on a wire rack to cool.

8 Make the buttercream (see page 51). Spread some on the flat side of a sponge. Gently press another one on top. Make more pies in the same way.

This buttercream was tinted with food dye and piped using a star-shaped nozzle (see page 27).

Sifted cocoa powder

Roll a pie over a plate of chocolate drops or sugar sprinkles, to make it look like this.

Drizzled melted chocolate (see page 56)

This pie was rolled in chopped nuts.

Mini cheesecakes

Ingredients:

175g (6oz) digestive biscuits

75g (3oz) butter

450g (1lb) full-fat cream cheese

125g (4½oz) caster sugar

2 large eggs

2 teaspoons of vanilla essence

For the topping:

½ lemon

4 tablespoons of smooth apricot jam

2 ripe peaches or nectarines

You will also need a 12-hole deep muffin tray and 12 paper muffin cases

Makes 12

These little cheesecakes are topped with sliced peaches or nectarines, but you could use 150g (5oz) fresh raspberries or blueberries instead, and swap the apricot jam in the topping for raspberry jam.

1 Heat the oven to 150°C, 300°F, gas mark 2. Put the paper cases in the tray.

2 Put the biscuits in a clean plastic food bag. Seal the end with an elastic band.

3 Roll a rolling pin over the bag to crush the biscuits into small pieces.

4 Melt the butter in a saucepan over a low heat. Mix in the biscuit crumbs.

5 Divide the mixture between the cases. Press it down with the back of a teaspoon.

6 Put the tray in the fridge to chill while you make the filling.

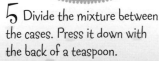

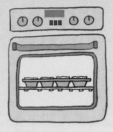

7 Put the cream cheese and sugar in a big bowl. Mix them together. Put the eggs and vanilla extract in a small bowl. Beat them with a fork.

8 Add the egg mixture to the cheese mixture a little at a time, beating well each time. Spoon the mixture into the cases.

9 Bake for 25 minutes. Turn off the oven and leave the tray in for another 30 minutes. Then, take it out.

10 Move the cheesecakes to a wire rack to cool. Put them in the fridge to chill for at least 2 hours. Then, make the topping.

11 Squeeze the juice from the lemon. Put it in a bowl and mix in the jam. Spread onto the cheesecakes.

12 Cut the peaches or nectarines in half, running the knife around the stone. Remove the stone. Cut the fruit into thin slices. Put them on the cheesecakes.

Remove the paper cases before you eat the cheesecakes.

Fruit toppings

Here are lots of ideas for decorating your cakes using fresh or dried fruit. Put some icing or buttercream on first, if you like.

Citrus zest

1 For tiny bits of zest, grate the outside of the fruit on the small holes of a grater.

Try not to grate the white layer underneath.

2 For strips of zest, it's easiest to use a zester. Scrape it across the fruit until you have long strips.

Glazed fruit

You will need enough fresh, glacé or dried fruit to decorate your cake, plus 4 tablespoons of smooth jam (such as raspberry or apricot) and 1 tablespoon of lemon juice.

1 Arrange the fruit on your cake. Put the jam and lemon juice in a bowl and mix.

2 Use a pastry brush to brush the glaze over the fruit.

Lime flavoured glacé icing (see page 38)

Glazed raspberries

Sugar-frosted redcurrants

Sugar-frosted fruit

You will need around 100g (4oz) fruit such as grapes, blueberries, strawberries or cherries, a sachet of dried egg white powder and around 4 tablespoons of caster sugar.

You will also need a small, new and clean paintbrush, some cocktail sticks and an orange.

1 Cut the orange in half. Put the halves on a big plate. Put a tablespoon of caster sugar in a small sieve.

2 Mix the egg white powder with water, following the instructions on the packet.

3 Use kitchen paper to dry the fruit. Push a piece onto a cocktail stick. Paint the egg white all over it using the paintbrush.

4 Sift the sugar over, turning the fruit so that every part of it is covered. Then, poke the end of the cocktail stick into an orange half.

5 Coat the rest of the fruit the same way. Leave to dry for 1-2 hours, or until the sugar is hard.

You can eat the oranges afterwards.

Sugar-frosted mint leaves

Decorate a cake with sliced fresh fruit such as strawberries or bananas.

Fresh fruit and whipped cream make a good topping or filling for a plain sponge cake.

23

Butterfly cakes

Ingredients:

For the cakes:
40g (1⅛oz) caster sugar
40g (1⅛oz) soft margarine
40g (1⅛oz) self-raising flour
1 medium egg
1½ teaspoons of cocoa powder

For the plain chocolate ganache:
40g (1⅛oz) plain or milk chocolate
2 tablespoons of double cream

For the white chocolate ganache:
60g (2⅛oz) white chocolate
2 tablespoons of double cream

You will also need:
25 mini paper cake cases
chocolate beans, sugar sprinkles
    and chocolate writing icing,
    to decorate

Makes about 25

These mini cakes are spread with a creamy chocolate topping called ganache, and the top of the cake is used to make wings shaped like a butterfly's. You can make bug-shaped cakes too, or just decorate your cakes with sugar sprinkles or chocolate buttons.

1 Heat the oven to 180°C, 350°F or gas mark 4. Arrange the paper cases on a baking tray.

2 Put the sugar and margarine in a big bowl. Sift in the flour. Break the egg into a cup, then pour it in. Mix it all together.

3 Spoon half the mixture into another bowl. Sift the cocoa powder over it. Mix it in.

Use two teaspoons, one to spoon and one to scrape.

Each case should be about half full.

4 Spoon the chocolate mixture into half the paper cases, and the vanilla mixture into the rest of the cases. Bake for 10-12 minutes, or until risen and firm.

5 Leave for a few minutes, then put on a wire rack to cool. Meanwhile, make the plain chocolate ganache and the white chocolate ganache (see page 56).

6 When the cakes are cold, take them out of their cases. Slice the top off each cake. Then, cut each top into 2 semicircles, like this.

Scatter on some sugar sprinkles, to decorate the butterfly's body.

7 Spread some ganache on top of each cake. Gently push 2 semicircles into the ganache on each cake, to make wings.

8 You could make a head from a chocolate bean and pipe on dots of chocolate writing icing for eyes.

To make a bug, put the wings on like this. You could pipe on dots, too.

Just spread on some ganache and top with a chocolate button.

Piping decorations

You can decorate cakes by squeezing, or piping, icing through a small hole or nozzle. Icing comes in tubes ready for piping, or you can buy a piping gun or bag, with different shaped nozzles. You can make your own icing and a simple piping bag.

Preparing cakes for piping

Pipe icing straight onto cakes, or on top of other toppings such as glacé icing or smooth buttercream.

Piping lines

You will need a tube, gun or bag with a round hole or nozzle, filled with buttercream (page 51), glacé icing (page 38) or bought icing.

1 Hold the tube, gun or bag over a cake and squeeze until a little icing comes out.

2 Move it across the cake, leaving a trail of icing in whatever shape you like.

3 For complicated shapes, use the end of a cocktail stick to draw on top of your cake first. Then, pipe over the patterns.

Piped decoration

Glacé icing

Add sweets or sugarpaste decorations.

This swirly topping was piped through a star-shaped nozzle.

Piping dots

Follow step 1 for piping lines on the opposite page. Squeeze until a dot forms. Then, lift the tube, gun or bag away quickly.

For two-tone buttercream, half fill a tube or gun with one shade, then fill it up with another shade. Some of the buttercream will mix.

A small swirl

Piping swirls

You will need a tube, gun or bag fitted with a star- or flower-shaped nozzle and filled with bought icing or home-made buttercream (page 51).

1 Hold the tube, gun or bag over a cake and squeeze until some icing comes out.

2 To pipe a small swirl, squeeze until a swirl forms. Stop squeezing and lift the nozzle away quickly.

Making a piping bag

You will need two plastic food bags and some buttercream (page 51) or glacé icing (page 38).

1 Tuck one food bag inside the other one. Spoon the icing into the inner bag.

2 Snip a tiny corner off the bags. Be careful the icing doesn't escape.

3 Follow the instructions for piping dots or piping lines.

3 To pipe a swirly topping, start piping at the edge of a cake. Keep squeezing as you move the nozzle in a spiral inwards and upwards. Then, lift the nozzle away quickly.

A piping bag

Macaroons

Ingredients:

100g (4oz) icing sugar
2 medium-sized eggs
a pinch of cream of tartar
¼ teaspoon of pink food dye
25g (1oz) caster sugar
100g (4oz) ground almonds

For the filling:

100g (4oz) fresh raspberries
150g (5oz) full-fat cream cheese
2 tablespoons of icing sugar

Makes about 12 pairs

Macaroons are made of whisked egg whites mixed with ground almonds and baked so the outside goes crisp while the inside stays chewy. To make them dairy-free, you can use a different filling – see the instructions on page 60.

1 Line two large baking sheets with baking parchment (see page 30). Sift the icing sugar into a bowl.

You don't need the yolks.

2 Separate the eggs (see page 5). Put the egg whites in a large, clean bowl.

3 Whisk the egg whites until they stand up in peaks (see page 5). Whisk in the cream of tartar, food dye and 2 tablespoons of the icing sugar.

4 Add the rest of the icing sugar a tablespoon at a time, whisking well each time.

Move the spoon in the shape of a number 8.

5 Add the caster sugar and ground almonds. Use a metal spoon to fold them in very gently.

Use another spoon to push the blob off.

6 Scoop up almost a teaspoon of the mixture. Put it on a tray. Make more blobs, spacing them out well.

7 Tap each tray sharply on the work surface, twice. Leave for 30 minutes.

This macaroon is lemon flavoured.

A mint chocolate macaroon

8 Heat the oven to 110°C, 225°F or gas mark ¼. Bake for 30 minutes. Turn off the oven. Leave the macaroons in for 15 minutes. Then leave them on the trays to cool.

9 To make the filling, mash the raspberries with a fork. Stir in the cream cheese and icing sugar.

A raspberry macaroon

10 Spread some filling on the flat side of a macaroon. Press on another macaroon. Fill the rest in the same way.

Lemon or orange macaroons

Use yellow food dye for lemon macaroons, or half yellow and half red for orange macaroons. For the filling, replace the raspberries with the grated rind of 1 orange or lemon; mix in 2 tablespoons of juice squeezed from the fruit and a few drops of food dye.

Mint chocolate macaroons

Replace the pink food dye with green and add 4 drops of peppermint essence at the same time. Instead of the raspberry filling, make some chocolate ganache – you'll find the recipe on page 56.

Tray cakes

All the cakes in this section are baked in trays and then cut into squares or slices. The tips you'll find here will help you when you're making tray cakes.

Sifting

Sometimes you need to sift dry ingredients through a sieve. Hold the sieve over a bowl and tap it. The ingredients will fall through. Squash any lumps through with the back of a spoon.

Greasing and lining tins and trays

Put the tin or tray on some baking parchment. Draw around it. Cut out the shape, cutting just inside the line. Wipe a little softened butter or cooking oil over the inside of the tin or tray, using a paper towel. Put the parchment shape in the bottom of the tin or tray.

Turning out tray cakes

Run a knife around the tray to loosen the cake. Put a wire rack over the tray. Turn the tray and rack over together, so the tray ends up on top. The cake should pop out onto the rack.

You can find out how to make decorations like these on pages 44-45.

Honey spice cake
– see pages 42-43

Cutting up tray cakes

The recipes in this section suggest roughly how many pieces to cut the cakes into, but this is only a guide. If you want to share a cake between more people, just cut smaller pieces.

Chocolate party cake
– see pages 40-41

Allergy-free tray cakes

Lots of the tray cakes in this section can be made allergy-free. There's a full list on pages 60-61.

Smoothing icing

When you're spreading icing or buttercream, dip the knife in warm water. The wet knife will slide over more easily.

There's a recipe for glacé icing, along with other sugar toppings, on page 38.

Lemon and mango loaf
– see pages 36-37

Cherry chocolate brownies

Ingredients:

100g (4oz) plain chocolate

2 large eggs

125g (4½oz) softened butter or soft margarine

275g (10oz) caster sugar

½ teaspoon of vanilla essence

50g (2oz) self-raising flour

25g (1oz) plain flour

2 tablespoons of cocoa powder

100g (4oz) dried cherries

100g (4oz) walnut or pecan pieces (optional)

You will also need a 20cm (8in) square cake tin

Makes 12 to 16

These brownies have a crispy top and a squidgy middle studded with nuts and cherries. You can leave out the nuts. Brownies taste good eaten warm with ice cream and chocolate sauce, made from the recipe opposite.

1 Heat the oven to 180°C, 350°F or gas mark 4. Grease and line the tray (see page 30).

2 Melt the chocolate, following the instructions on page 56.

3 Break the eggs into a small bowl. Beat them with a fork.

4 Put the butter or margarine, sugar and vanilla in a big bowl. Beat until they are fluffy. Add the eggs a little at a time, beating well each time.

5 Sift both types of flour and the cocoa powder into the bowl. Add the melted chocolate. Mix well.

6 Mix in the cherries and nuts. Scrape the mixture into the tin. Smooth the top with the back of a spoon.

The chocolate sauce goes hard on the cold ice cream.

You could cut up some fresh cherries to eat with your brownies. Cut them in half, running the knife around the central stone.

If you prefer more traditional brownies, just leave out the cherries.

Chocolate sauce

You will need 100g (4oz) chocolate drops, 2 tablespoons of golden syrup or honey and 1 tablespoon of water.

Put all the ingredients in a pan over a low heat. Stir until you have a glossy mixture. Leave to cool for a few minutes before eating.

7 Bake for 35 minutes, until slightly risen. It should have a crust on top but a soft middle.

Cut into 12-16 pieces

8 Leave in the tin for 20 minutes to cool.

Swiss roll

Swiss roll is a type of sponge cake baked in a tray, spread with a filling and then rolled up. This recipe has a raspberry filling, and both the cake and filling are dairy-free. There are other filling suggestions opposite.

1 Heat the oven to 200°C, 400°F or gas mark 6. Grease and line the tin (see page 30).

Don't worry if the outside cracks a little. That's how it's supposed to look.

Cut the roll into sli[ces]

2 Break the eggs into a big bowl. Add the sugar. Beat until the mixture is pale and thick.

3 Sift over half the flour, then fold it in gently, using a big metal spoon. Sift over the rest of the flour, add the water and fold everything together again.

4 Pour the mixture into the tray. Push it into the corners and smooth the top with the back of a spoon. Bake for 10-12 minutes, or until pale golden and springy.

5 Cut a piece of baking parchment slightly bigger than the tray. Lay it out and scatter the caster sugar over it. Run a knife around the tin.

6 Wearing oven gloves, turn the cake onto the parchment. Peel the old parchment off. Carefully roll up the cake from a short end, with the new parchment inside. Leave to cool.

7 For the filling, put the raspberries in a bowl. Use a fork or potato masher to mash them. Mix in the jam.

8 When the cake is cool, carefully unroll it. Spread over the filling, then roll it up again, without the parchment.

Buttercream fillings

Instead of the fruit filling here, you could use vanilla buttercream and spread on 2 tablespoons of jam.

Whipped cream fillings

Choose one of the flavoured whipped creams on page 50, or open a 400g (14oz) can of cherries or crushed pineapple, drain the fruit and stir it gently into 300ml (½ pint) whipped cream.

Lemon and mango loaf

Ingredients:

150g (5oz) dried mango

2 lemons

100g (4oz) caster sugar

75g (3oz) butter, softened

75g (3oz) ground almonds

300ml (½ pint) natural yogurt

2 teaspoons of vanilla essence

250g (9oz) plain flour

2 teaspoons of bicarbonate of soda

For the lemon glacé icing:

175g (6oz) icing sugar

about 1 tablespoon of lemon juice

You will also need:

a 900g (2lb) loaf tin, measuring about 20½ x 12½ x 8cm (8 x 5 x 3½in)

Makes 12 slices

This fruity loaf cake contains lemon juice and zest and dried mango, and is covered in sticky lemon icing. There are other combinations of fruit to try too – see the opposite page. This recipe is egg-free.

1 Heat the oven to 180°C, 350°F, or gas mark 4. Snip the mango into small pieces. Grease and line the tin (see page 30).

2 Grate the zest from the lemons (see page 22). Put it in a big bowl. Cut one lemon in half and squeeze the juice from one half. Put the juice aside.

3 Put the butter and sugar in the big bowl. Beat until pale and fluffy.

4 Stir in the ground almonds, 4 rounded tablespoons of the yogurt and the vanilla. Sift over the flour and bicarbonate of soda. Add the remaining yogurt and the mango.

Move the spoon in the shape of a number 8.

6 Scrape the mixture into the tin. Bake for 45-50 minutes, or until lightly browned and firm.

5 Fold the mixture together gently, using a large metal spoon. Stop when all the flour is mixed in.

You could use extra chopped mango to decorate the top of the loaf.

7 Leave the cake in the tin for 10 minutes, then turn it onto a wire rack. Turn it the right way up, then leave it to cool.

8 Use the juice you set aside earlier to make the lemon glacé icing (see page 38). Use a blunt knife to spread the icing onto the cold cake.

Lemon and sultana loaf

Replace the mango with sultanas – or use dried blueberries.

Lime and fig loaf

Replace the lemons with 4 limes and the mango with dried figs – or use dates.

Orange and cherry loaf

Replace the lemons with oranges and the mango with dried sour cherries – or use dried apricots.

Sugar toppings

Sugar can be used to make different types of icings, and as a decoration in itself. Here are some recipes and ideas for different ways of using sugar.

Glacé icing

To ice a big cake or a batch of cupcakes, you will need 175g (6oz) icing sugar, some food dye (optional) and 1½ tablespoons of warm water.

Sift the icing sugar into a bowl. Mix in a few drops of food dye and the water.

Plain glacé icing

Coloured glacé icing

Lime glacé icing decorated with lime zest (see page 22)

Citrus glacé icing

Leave out the food dye, if you like, and replace the water with orange, lemon or lime juice. Stir in 1 teaspoon of finely grated citrus zest (optional).

Feather icing

You will need some glacé icing, bought writing icing and a cocktail stick.

1 Spread the glacé icing over a cake. Before it dries, pipe lines across it (see page 26) with the writing icing.

2 Drag the point of the cocktail stick across the lines. Move it along. Drag it across the lines in the opposite direction. Do this again and again.

This type of feather icing was made by piping dots of writing icing, then dragging a cocktail cocktail stick through them.

This feather icing was done with different shades of writing icing.

Stencilling with icing sugar

You will need some cocktail sticks, some icing sugar, a sieve and a lacy doily – or you could make your own stencil by cutting shapes from a piece of paper.

1 Lay the stencil over the cake. Stick a few cocktail sticks through the holes, to keep it still.

The stencil should be bigger than the cake.

2 Sift a thin layer of icing sugar over the cake. Remove the cocktail sticks and carefully lift off the stencil.

Stencilled pattern made with a lacy doily

Bought sugar sprinkles and sweets make good cake decorations, too.

Coloured sugar

You will need some granulated sugar and some food dye.

1 Put 1 tablespoon of sugar on a plate. Mix in a few drops of food dye. Spread it out and leave it for about 2 hours.

You could sprinkle coloured sugar through a stencil. This cake was decorated using a dotty stencil.

2 When the sugar has dried, crush any lumps with the back of a spoon. Then, sprinkle it onto iced cakes.

Chocolate party cake

Ingredients:

100g (4oz) self-raising flour

40g (1½oz) cocoa powder

1½ teaspoons of baking powder

150g (5oz) softened butter or
　　soft margarine

150g (5oz) soft brown sugar

1 teaspoon of vanilla essence

3 tablespoons of milk

3 large eggs

For the chocolate buttercream:

100g (4oz) softened unsalted
　　butter or margarine

175g (6oz) icing sugar

40g (1½oz) cocoa powder

1 tablespoon of milk

½ teaspoon of vanilla essence

You will also need a 27 x 18cm
　　(11 x 7in) rectangular cake tin

Makes 12 - 15 squares

This chocolate cake can be cut up into lots of squares so it's great for handing around at parties. The cake shown here is decorated with chocolate beans and drizzled white chocolate, but you can use any decorations you like.

1 Heat the oven to 180°C, 350°F or gas mark 4. Grease and line the tin (see page 30).

2 Sift the flour, cocoa and baking powder into a big bowl. Put the butter and sugar in another bowl.

3 Beat the butter or margarine and sugar until pale and fluffy. Mix in the vanilla and milk.

4 Crack an egg into a cup. Tip it into the butter and sugar mixture. Add 1 tablespoon of the floury mixture. Beat well. Do this with each egg.

Move the spoon in the

shape of a number 8.

5 Add the rest of the floury mixture and stir it in gently, using a big metal spoon.

6 Scrape the mixture into the tin and level the top with the back of a spoon. Bake for 30-35 minutes, until risen and springy.

It will be easier to cut your cake if you take out any candles first, too.

If you tie a ribbon around the cake, remember to take it off before you cut the cake.

7 When the cake is cooked, leave it in the tin for a few minutes, then turn it out onto a wire rack (see page 30).

Peel off the parchment.

8 To make the chocolate buttercream, see page 51.

9 When the cake is cold, spread the buttercream over the top.

10 Decorate with drizzled chocolate (see page 56), chocolate beans and candles too, if you like. To eat, cut into 12 or 15 squares.

Honey spice cake

Ingredients:

1 lemon

1 orange

150g (5oz) soft light brown sugar

150g (5oz) softened butter or soft margarine

3 medium eggs

2 teaspoons of baking powder

150g (5oz) semolina or fine cornmeal (polenta)

2 teaspoons of ground cinnamon

½ teaspoon of ground allspice

150g (5oz) ground almonds

4 tablespoons of runny honey

You will also need:

a 27 x 18cm (11 x 7in) rectangular cake tray

ready-to-roll icing, marzipan or sugarpaste and extra honey, to decorate (optional)

Makes 12 - 15 squares

This sticky cake tastes of honey, cinnamon and lemon. You can make it wheat- and gluten-free by using cornmeal instead of the semolina. You can also make it dairy-free – you'll find instructions on page 61.

1 Heat the oven to 180°C, 350°F or gas mark 4. Grease and line the tray (see page 30).

2 Squeeze the juice from the orange and lemon. Put it in a jug.

3 Put the sugar and butter or margarine in a big bowl. Beat until you have a pale and fluffy mixture.

4 Break an egg into a bowl and beat it. Stir it into the mixture in the big bowl. Do the same with the other eggs. Don't worry if it looks lumpy.

5 Put the baking powder, semolina or cornmeal, cinnamon, allspice and ground almonds in a bowl and mix. Tip them into the large bowl.

6 Add 4 tablespoons of juice from the jug and stir. Scrape the mixture into the tray and level the top with the back of a spoon. Bake for 30-35 minutes.

You could decorate your cake with flowers and bees made from sugarpaste or marzipan – see pages 44-45.

To stick decorations to the cake, brush a dab of honey on the back of each one, then press it onto the cake.

Don't worry if it doesn't all mix in.

7 Meanwhile, put the honey in the jug and mix it in. When the cake is risen and firm, take it out of the oven.

8 Give the mixture in the jug a stir, then pour it over the cake. Leave the cake in the tray to cool, then cut it into 12-15 squares.

Honey spice cupcakes

At step 1, heat the oven to 200°C, 400°F or gas mark 6. Line a 12-hole deep muffin tray with 12 paper cases. Follow steps 2-5. At step 6, spoon the mixture into the cases and bake for 15-20 minutes. Follow the rest of the steps.

Making decorations

You can make your own colourful cake decorations from bought ready-to-roll icing, bought marzipan or home-made sugarpaste.

These decorations were pressed into some whipped cream.

A button shape

Sugarpaste

You will need a sachet of dried egg white powder, 1 lemon and 250g (9oz) icing sugar.

1 Make up the egg white powder with water, following the instructions on the packet. Squeeze the juice from the lemon. Sift the icing sugar into a big bowl.

2 Put 2½ teaspoons of egg white mixture and 1 tablespoon of lemon juice in the bowl. Use a blunt knife to cut through the mixture, until it starts to mix.

3 Squeeze the mixture until it clings together in a smooth ball. To colour it, follow the instructions on the right for colouring marzipan.

Balls of sugarpaste

Colouring marzipan

You will need a block of bought 'white' marzipan and some food dye. (Marzipan contains nuts.)

1 Put a golf-ball sized blob of marzipan in a bowl. Make a hollow in the middle and drop in 1 or 2 drops of food dye.

2 Fold the marzipan over the dye. Keep folding and squashing the marzipan until the colour is evenly mixed through.

Cutting decorations

1 Dust a surface and rolling pin with icing sugar. Roll out the ready-to-roll icing, marzipan or sugarpaste until it is half as thin as your little finger.

2 Use little cookie cutters to cut out shapes. Squeeze the scraps together, roll them out and cut out more shapes.

Moulding decorations

To make balls, roll a piece of ready-to-roll icing, sugarpaste or marzipan between the palms of your hands, like this.

To press dots or stripes into ready-to-roll icing, sugarpaste or marzipan, press the end or side of a cocktail stick into it.

To make a button shape, cut a circle the size of a button. Press a clean, new button onto it. Remove the button.

To stick a decoration to a cake, brush the back of it with a little jam or honey.

This bird was cut out using a small leaf-shaped cutter.

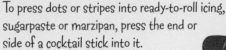

To join shapes, press them together while they are still moist.

These marks were made with a cocktail stick.

Cover a cupcake with a circle or flower shape cut from sugarpaste, marzipan or ready-to-roll icing.

Big cakes

Big cakes can look spectacular, and they aren't difficult to make as long as you follow the recipe carefully. The tips here will help you when you're making the cakes in this section.

Allergy-free big cakes

Lots of the big cakes in this section can be made allergy free. See page 61 for suggestions.

Greasing and lining tins

Follow the instructions for greasing and lining trays on page 30.

To find out about fruit toppings, see pages 22-23.

A plain sponge cake filled with jam and cream — see pages 48-49

Several of the cakes in this section have layers sandwiched together with a filling.

Removing big cakes from tins

To remove a loose-bottomed cake tin, put the tin over a full food can. Undo any clips on the tin. Push the sides of the tin down around the can. You can see how to do this on page 55.

To remove an ordinary tin, hold it upside down over a wire rack and shake it gently. The cake should pop out. If it doesn't, run a knife around between the tin and the cake, to loosen it, then try again.

Moving big cakes

Lifting a big cake onto a plate or stand can be tricky. It's best to slide the cake slowly across onto the plate or stand from the wire rack.

Always move cakes onto their plates or stands before you pile on extra layers, toppings or decorations - it's harder to move the cake after you've done this.

Slices of cake

The easiest way to move a slice of cake onto a plate is to use a cake server. Slide the blade under the slice of cake, then lift it up and put it on a plate. Gently pull out the blade from under the cake.

Find out how to whip cream and make other creamy toppings and fillings on page 50.

Cream cheese frosting – see page 51

Pineapple pecan cake scattered with pecan nut pieces – see page 53

Sponge cake

Ingredients:

225g (8oz) self-raising flour
225g (8oz) caster sugar
225g (8oz) soft margarine
4 medium eggs

For the buttercream filling:
100g (4oz) softened butter or
    soft margarine
225g (8oz) icing sugar
1 tablespoon of milk
½ teaspoon of vanilla essence
a few drops of food colouring

You will also need two 20cm (8in)
    round, shallow cake tins

Makes 12 slices

Sponge cake is simple to make and very adaptable.
The main recipe here is for a plain, 2-layer sponge
cake sandwiched with buttercream, but there
are suggestions for other fillings, and different
flavours of sponge too.

1 Heat the oven to 180°C, 350°F or gas mark 4. Grease and line
the tins (see page 30).

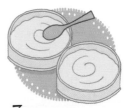

2 Sift the flour into a big
bowl. Add the sugar and
margarine. Break an egg into
a cup, then tip it into the
bowl. Do the same with the
other eggs.

3 Stir until you have
smooth mixture. Spoon
half into each cake tin
and smooth the tops with
the back of the spoon.

4 Bake for 25
minutes, or until the
cakes are risen and
firm. Leave in the
tins for 5 minutes.

5 Run a knife around the
tins, then turn the cakes onto
a wire rack (see page 47).

6 Peel off the parchment. Turn the
cakes the right way up. Then, make
the buttercream (see page 51).

7 When the cakes are cool,
put one on a plate, flat
side up. Spread on the
buttercream. Put the other
cake on top, flat side down.
Press gently. Sprinkle some
caster sugar on top.

Other flavours of sponge

Chocolate sponge
Replace 40g (1½oz) of the flour with cocoa powder.

Coffee sponge
Mix 1 rounded tablespoon of instant coffee with 1 tablespoon of hot water. Cool and add after step 2.

Citrus sponge
Grate the zest of 2 lemons, limes or oranges and add it after step 2.

Sugar and spice sponge
Add 2 teaspoons of ground cinnamon and 1 teaspoon of ground ginger at step 2. This goes well with a vanilla buttercream filling.

Other fillings

Jam and buttercream
Spread 4 tablespoons of jam on top of the buttercream at step 7.

Fruity filling
For a dairy-free raspberry filling, see the Swiss roll recipe on pages 34-35.

Creamy fillings
Use the flavoured buttercreams on page 51, or 150ml (¼ pint) whipped cream (see page 50). You could spread on 4 tablespoons of jam before the cream.

Fruit creams
You could fill your cake with raspberry or citrus cream (see page 50).

Lemon sponge filled with lemon buttercream

Plain sponge filled with jam and buttercream

Chocolate sponge filled with raspberry cream

Creamy toppings

These recipes make enough to top or fill a big cake. To top and fill a cake, double the quantities – but each recipe will tell you how much you need for that particular cake.

Whipped cream

You will need 150ml (¼ pint) of double or whipping cream.

Don't beat too much, or the cream will go hard.

1 Pour the cream into a large bowl. Hold the bowl firmly. Beat the cream with a whisk as quickly as you can.

2 Beat until the cream becomes stiff. When you lift the whisk, the cream should stand up in a floppy point.

Vanilla cream

Add ½ teaspoon of vanilla essence and sift over 1 tablespoon of icing sugar, before you whip the cream.

Raspberry cream

Mash 125g (4½oz) fresh raspberries with a fork. Stir in 1½ tablespoons of caster sugar. Stir into the whipped cream gently, using a metal spoon.

Instead of raspberries, you could use the same weight of fresh blackberries.

Citrus cream

Grate the zest from 1 lime or ½ orange or ½ lemon. Stir it into the whipped cream gently, with 1½ tablespoons of sifted icing sugar.

Buttercream

Orange buttercream

You will need 100g (4oz) softened, unsalted butter or soft margarine, 225g (8oz) icing sugar, 1 tablespoon of milk, ½ teaspoon of vanilla essence and some food dye (optional).

1 Put the butter or margarine in a large mixing bowl and beat with a wooden spoon until it becomes soft and fluffy.

2 Sift one third of the icing sugar into the bowl and stir it in. Then, sift the rest of the icing sugar over the mixture.

3 Add the milk and vanilla. Beat quickly, until you have a pale and fluffy mixture.

You could mix in a few drops of food dye too, to tint your buttercream.

For extra tang, add a teaspoon of finely grated citrus zest to make citrus buttercream.

Chocolate buttercream

Use just 175g (6oz) icing sugar and sift in 40g (1½oz) cocoa powder at the same time. Leave out the food dye.

Citrus buttercream

Replace the milk and vanilla with the finely grated rind from 1 orange, 1 lemon or 2 limes, and 2 teaspoons of juice from the fruit.

Cream cheese frosting

You will need 50g (2oz) icing sugar, 200g (7oz) full fat cream cheese at room temperature and 1 tablespoon of lemon juice.

Sift the icing sugar into a large bowl. Add the cream cheese and lemon juice. Mix gently.

Don't beat too hard, or the frosting will go thin and watery.

Pineapple cake

Ingredients:

For the cake:

250g (9oz) plain flour

2 teaspoons of baking powder

125g (4½oz) soft dark brown sugar

2 teaspoons of ground cinnamon

150ml (¼ pint) sunflower or vegetable oil

3 large eggs

1 teaspoon of vanilla essence

a 400g (14oz) can of crushed pineapple

For the cream cheese frosting:

400g (14oz) full-fat cream cheese, at room temperature

150g (5oz) icing sugar

You will also need:

2 x 20cm (8in) round, shallow cake tins

dried pineapple pieces, to decorate

Makes 12 slices

This moist, light cake is made using canned crushed pineapple. It's filled and topped with cream cheese frosting flavoured with pineapple juice and pieces.

1 Heat the oven to 180°C, 350°F or gas mark 4. Grease and line the tins (see page 30).

Beat the oil mixture with a fork.

2 Put the flour, baking powder, sugar and cinnamon in a large bowl. Mix. Put the oil in another bowl. Break each egg into a cup. Add it to the oil, with the vanilla.

3 Put 2 tablespoons of pineapple in a small bowl. Add the rest to the oil and egg mixture. Stir it in.

4 Mix the oil mixture into the flour mixture. Divide between the cake tins. Bake for 25 minutes, until risen and golden brown.

Stir very gently.

Peel off the baking parchment and leave the cakes to cool completely.

5 Leave the cakes in their tins for 10 minutes. Then, turn them out onto a wire rack.

6 Make the cream cheese frosting (see page 51). Mix in the pineapple you set aside earlier.

Contains nuts

Pineapple pecan cake

For a nutty version, follow steps 1-3, then add 50g (2oz) pecan or walnut pieces to the oil mixture. Follow steps 4-8. Decorate the top with pecan or walnut halves or pieces.

7 When the cakes are cold, put one on a plate, flat side down. Spread over half the frosting. Put the other cake on top, flat side down. Spread on the remaining frosting.

Arrange the dried pineapple pieces on top of the cake.

Make swirls in the frosting as you spread it on.

Don't worry if your cakes look a little uneven – the frosting will cover up any bumps.

Coffee cake

Ingredients:

2 dessertspoons of instant coffee granules

175g (6oz) softened butter or soft margarine

175g (6oz) caster sugar

3 large eggs

175g (6oz) self-raising flour

1½ teaspoons of baking powder

200g (7oz) walnut or pecan pieces (optional)

For the buttercream:

175g (6oz) softened butter or soft margarine

200g (7oz) icing sugar

You will also need a 20cm (8in) spring-clip cake tin

Makes 12 slices

This coffee cake can be cut it in half and filled and topped with coffee buttercream. If you don't want to cut it in half, just leave the cake whole, make half the amount of buttercream and spread it on top. Leave out the nuts if you prefer.

1 Heat the oven to 180°C, 350°F or gas mark 4. Grease and line the tin (see page 30).

2 Put the coffee granules in a cup and add 2 dessertspoons of boiling water. Mix.

3 Put the butter or margarine and sugar in a big bowl. Beat until the mixture is pale and fluffy. Break the eggs into a bowl and beat them with a fork.

4 Add a spoonful of egg to the buttery mixture and stir it in. Add the rest of the egg a spoonful at a time, mixing well each time.

5 Sift the flour and baking powder over the bowl. Stir them in. Add half the coffee and the nuts. Mix well.

6 Scrape the mixture into the tin. Smooth the top with the back of a spoon. Bake for 30-35 minutes, until firm. Leave in the tin for 10 minutes to cool slightly.

7 Put the tin over a full food can. Undo the clip on the tin. Push the sides of the tin down around the can.

8 Carefully slide the cake off the base of the tin, onto a wire rack. Leave it to cool completely.

9 When the cake is cold, cut it into two layers. Steady the cake gently with one hand and cut very carefully with a sharp knife.

Scatter extra nuts over the top of your cake, if you like.

10 Make the coffee buttercream, following the instructions on the right.

11 Spread half the buttercream on the bottom layer. Put the top back on and spread the rest of the buttercream over it.

Coffee buttercream

Put the butter or margarine in a big bowl. Beat it with a wooden spoon until it becomes soft and fluffy. Sift over one third of the icing sugar and stir it in. Then, sift the rest of the icing sugar over the mixture. Add the rest of the coffee. Beat quickly, until you have a pale and fluffy mixture.

Chocolate toppings

Here you'll find recipes for some delicious chocolate toppings to spread on, or in, your cakes, as well as ideas for chocolate decorations. And, if you want to make chocolate buttercream, you'll find a recipe on page 51.

For cooking, you can use chocolate drops or chunks of chocolate from a bar.

Melting chocolate

1 Put the chocolate in a heatproof bowl. Fill a pan a quarter full of water and put it over a medium heat.

When the water bubbles, take the pan off the heat.

2 Carefully lower the bowl into the pan. Leave for 5 minutes, then stir the chocolate until it is all melted.

Drizzling chocolate

1 Melt 75g (3oz) plain, milk or white chocolate (see above).

2 Scoop up some melted chocolate. Hold the spoon over a cake. Tip the spoon, then move it over the cake, leaving a trail of chocolate.

This cake was drizzled with plain chocolate, then white chocolate.

Chocolate ganache

Ganache is a creamy, chocolatey filling or topping. You will need 40g (1½oz) plain or milk chocolate (or 60g (2½oz) white chocolate) and 2 tablespoons of double cream.

1 Melt the chocolate (see above). Stir in the cream. Lift the bowl out of the pan.

2 Let it cool for 10 minutes, then put it in the fridge for 1 hour. Stir every now and then.

Plain chocolate ganache

Chocolate curls

You will need a bar of cooking chocolate that's at room temperature.

Scrape strips from the side of the bar using a vegetable peeler.

For bigger curls, scrape chocolate from underneath the bar.

Small curls →

← *Big curl*

You could make a topping of raspberries and chocolate curls for the chocolate layer cake on pages 58-59.

When you put chocolate leaves on a cake, touch them as little as possible, or they will melt.

Chocolate leaves

You will need 100g (4oz) plain chocolate, about 15 fresh mint leaves, a baking tray lined with baking parchment and a small, new and clean paintbrush.

1 Melt the chocolate (see the opposite page). Use the paintbrush to paint the chocolate onto the backs of the mint leaves, in a thick layer.

Don't paint the stalks.

Make more than you need, in case some break later on.

2 Put the leaves on the tray with the chocolate side up. Refrigerate for 45 minutes, or until the chocolate has set.

3 Use a cocktail stick to flip over each leaf, so the chocolate faces down.

4 Hold the chocolate down with the cocktail stick. Grasp the stalk and gently peel off each mint leaf.

Chocolate layer cake

This light, chocolatey layer cake is filled with jam and cream and topped with fruit. You can easily make it wheat- and gluten-free or dairy-free – see page 61 for suggestions.

Ingredients:

For the filling:

4 large eggs

125g (4½oz) caster sugar

60g (2½oz) ground almonds

1½ tablespoons of cocoa powder

1¼ teaspoons of baking powder

For the filling:

300ml (½ pint) double or whipping cream

3 tablespoons of jam

To decorate:

about 150g (5oz) fresh fruit, such as raspberries, blueberries and strawberries.

1 tablespoon of icing sugar

You will also need 3 x 18cm (7in) round, shallow cake tins

Makes 8-10 slices

1 Heat the oven to 180°C, 350°F or gas mark 4. Grease and line the tins (see page 30).

2 Separate the eggs (see page 5), so the whites are in one bowl and the yolks are in another. Add the sugar to the yolks.

3 Mix the yolks and sugar with a fork. Stir in the ground almonds, cocoa powder and baking powder.

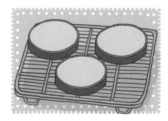

6 Bake for 15-20 minutes, until firm and springy. Leave in the tins for 10 minutes. Then, turn them onto a wire rack to cool. When the cakes are cold, whip the cream.

4 Beat the egg whites with a whisk until they stand up in floppy points (see page 5).

Move the spoon in the shape of a number 8.

5 Spoon the egg whites into the egg yolk mixture. Fold them in gently, using a metal spoon. Spoon the mixture into the tins.

To decorate your layer cake with chocolate leaves, see page 57.

Choose a flavour of jam that goes with the fruit you're using.

Instead of berries, you could use sliced peaches, cherries, kiwi fruit or pineapple.

7 Peel off the parchment. Put a cake on a plate. Spread on half the jam and a third of the cream.

8 Put another cake gently on top. Carefully, spread over the remaining jam and half the remaining cream.

9 Put the final cake on top. Spread over the remaining cream.

10 Arrange the fruit on top. Sift over the icing sugar.

2-layer cake

Instead of 3 x 18cm (7in) cake tins, you can use 2 x 20cm (8in) round, shallow tins. Bake for 20-25 minutes. Divide the jam and cream between the 2 layers.

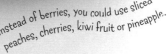

Allergy advice

Here you can find out which recipes are suitable for people with particular allergies or food intolerances. There are also suggestions for adapting recipes, for example by using dairy-free spread instead of butter (other substitutions, such as using gluten-free flour, might not work). Check packaged ingredients, such as vanilla essence and cocoa powder, in case they contain anything unsuitable. And if you're baking with dairy-free spread, avoid low-fat types.

 Marbled muffins   pages 8-9

Contain wheat, gluten, dairy and eggs.
Dairy-free option: replace the milk with soya milk and use dairy-free chocolate.

 Little banana cakes   pages 10-11

Contain wheat, gluten, dairy, eggs and nuts.
Dairy-free option: use dairy-free spread and replace the frosting with glacé icing (page 38).
Nut-free option: leave out the nuts.

 Vanilla cupcakes   pages 12-13

Contain wheat, gluten, dairy and eggs.
Dairy-free option: use dairy-free spread for the cakes and use dairy-free spread and soya milk for the buttercream.

 Orange drizzle cupcakes   pages 14-15

Contain dairy and eggs.
Dairy-free option: use dairy-free spread.

 Strawberry shortcakes   pages 16-17

Contain wheat, gluten, dairy and eggs.

 Whoopie pies   pages 18-19

Contain wheat, gluten, dairy and eggs.

 Mini cheesecakes   pages 20-21

Contain wheat, gluten, dairy and eggs.
Wheat- and gluten-free option: use wheat- and gluten-free biscuits.

 Butterfly cakes   pages 24-25

Contain wheat, gluten, dairy and eggs.
Dairy-free option: use dairy-free spread and dairy-free cocoa powder for the cakes; replace the ganache with chocolate buttercream made with dairy-free spread and soya milk (page 51).

 Macaroons   pages 28-29

Contain dairy, eggs and nuts.
Dairy-free option: replace the filling with the raspberry filling on pages 34-35.

 Cherry chocolate brownies   pages 32-33

Contain wheat, gluten, dairy, eggs and nuts.
Dairy-free option: use dairy-free spread, dairy-free cocoa powder and dairy-free chocolate for the brownies and dairy-free chocolate for the sauce.
Nut-free option: leave out the nuts.

 Swiss roll   pages 34-35

Contains wheat, gluten and eggs.

Lemon and mango loaf   pages 36-37

Contains wheat, gluten, dairy and nuts.

 Chocolate party cake   pages 40-41

Contains wheat, gluten, dairy and eggs.
Dairy-free option: use dairy-free spread,
dairy-free cocoa powder and soya milk for
the cake and for the buttercream.

 Honey spice cake   pages 42-43

Contains wheat, gluten, dairy, eggs and nuts.
Wheat- and gluten-free option: use cornmeal.
Dairy-free option: use dairy-free spread.

 Sponge cake   pages 48-49

Contains wheat, gluten, dairy, eggs and nuts.
Dairy-free option: use dairy-free spread and choose
a dairy-free filling such as vanilla buttercream made
with dairy-free spread and soya milk.

 Pineapple cake   pages 52-53

Contains wheat, gluten, dairy and eggs.
Dairy-free option: replace the cream cheese
frosting with vanilla buttercream made with
dairy-free spread and soya milk.

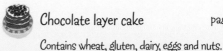 Coffee cake   pages 54-55

Contains wheat, gluten, dairy, eggs and nuts.
Dairy-free option: use dairy-free spread for the
cake and for the buttercream.
Nut-free option: leave out the nuts.

Chocolate layer cake   pages 56-57

Contains wheat, gluten, dairy, eggs and nuts.
Wheat- and gluten-free option: use wheat- and
gluten-free cocoa powder and wheat- and
gluten-free baking powder.
Dairy-free option: use dairy-free cocoa powder and
replace the filling with chocolate buttercream made with
dairy-free spread, dairy-free cocoa powder and soya milk.

Toppings, fillings and decorations

 Fruit toppings   pages 22-23
Free from wheat, gluten, dairy, eggs and nuts.

 Sugar toppings   pages 38-39
Free from wheat, gluten, dairy, eggs and nuts.

 Sugarpaste   page 44
Contains egg.

Whipped cream   page 50
Contains dairy.

Cream cheese frosting   page 51
Contains dairy.

 Buttercream   page 51
Contains dairy.
Dairy-free option: use dairy-free spread and soya
milk or water.
Use allergy-free cocoa powder for the chocolate
buttercream, if necessary.

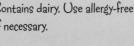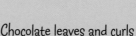 Chocolate ganache   page 56
Contains dairy. Use allergy-free chocolate
if necessary.

Chocolate leaves and curls   page 57
Use allergy-free chocolate if necessary.

Index

Edited by Jane Chisholm

Art Director: Mary Cartwright

Digital imaging: Nick Wakeford

Food preparation by Dagmar Vesely

With thanks to Emily Bone and Fiona Patchett

This edition first published in 2013 by Usborne Publishing Ltd., 83-85 Saffron Hill, London EC1N 8RT, England. www.usborne.com Copyright © 2013, 2010 Usborne Publishing Limited. The name Usborne and the devices ♀⊕ are Trade Marks of Usborne Publishing Ltd. All rights reserved. No part of this publication may be reproduced, stored in a retrieval system, or transmitted in any form or by any means, electronic, mechanical, photocopying, recording or otherwise, without the prior permission of the publisher. UKE. Printed in China.